Table

Canva Tips and Tricks Beyond The Limits

Koushik K

KOUSHIK K

First of All, Thank you for purchasing this guide

If you are a professional designer, you may be having Photoshop or similar designing software to produce your graphics, but still, you may not deny the fact that Canva is a hundred times easier and quicker to do with when it comes to designing wonderful stuff.

For hobby designers or newbies, Canva is like a great gift because of its user-friendly, self-explanatory, and easy interface. I once taught Canva to a friend who was never inclined towards graphic design and now, he uses it full time to produce graphics for work and personal purposes. Therefore, I am sure that Canva is one of the best web applications there is for producing sophisticated designs easily either for social media or even for print in some cases. (unless you want to print large posters etc. for which vector images would be the best fit.) Canva's core advantage is that it has a very little learning curve.

This book is not going to concentrate much on the basics of Canva because there are many tutorials available for that. This book will mainly deal with the limitations of Canva and how to deal with them (Legally)

If you are eager to know what those limitations are before moving forward to further discussions, you can have a glance at the table of contents of this book. My aim is to find workable solutions to those real limitations and give you a working solution.

So, Let's start...

The Basics

For this book, I will be using the web version of Canva for demonstration, because I find it easy and more efficient for designing than the mobile version. However, there is a mobile version of Canva app available for you if you prefer designing with your mobile.

Find the details needed in Canva.com

You can skip this chapter if you are already using Canva.

https://www.skillshare.com/classes/Getting-Started-with-Canva-for-Beginners-CANVA-BASICS-1/740963239?via=browse-rating-Canva-layout-grid[1]

Canva basics – just signup to a free skillshare account and access this course (if you need it)

P.S – don't worry, it was not an affiliate link, just a direct link to a useful resource.

I assume you brought this book because you already know the basics, and you just want to learn some more tricks in Canva. In that case, just move forward....

NOW LET'S START WITH ALL THE STUFF THAT THEY DON'T TEACH YOU IN THE BASICS

---

1. https://www.skillshare.com/classes/Getting-Started-with-Canva-for-Beginners-CANVA-BASICS-1/740963239?via=browse-rating-canva-layout-grid

Background remover and exporting Transparent GIFs

Canva pro offers a filter called background remover for paid users of Canva. Let us discuss a popular workaround now

Remove.BG

https://www.remove.bg/

You have to visit the above link and sign up

The only limitation of this website is that you can only download low-quality preview images (low-resolution images) for Free

(I will teach you how to change the resolution to a high resolution in an upcoming chapter)

Now let's see how to remove backgrounds for your images using this free service.

After signing up, log in to your account

Step 1: Login and click the remove background button on the website, then click the upload image button

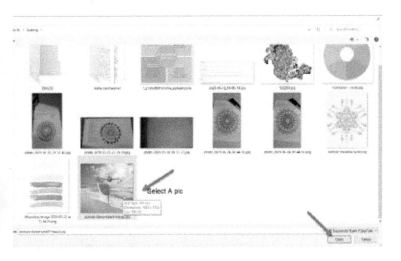

Step 2: Select the file you wish to remove the background from and click open.

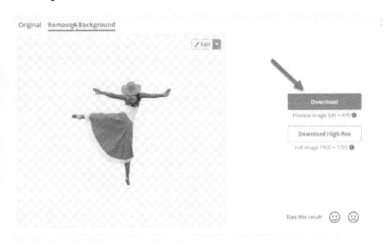

Step 3: Click the blue download button and save the file.

Note: the website offers you premium paid services, but I feel a free account is sufficient for what we will be doing.

That's it for this chapter. You can explore the site for more features.

https://www.remove.bg/

Paste design elements from one design to another

There is a pro feature inside folders—>all your designs, which lets you select any design you, want to paste inside the current working design and edit the elements.

We have a workaround that works in the desktop version, while using the web version of Canva, I don't have a similar workaround for mobile apps. I will update you if I find one.

You may already know that you can log in to multiple tabs with the same account login in your browser. We can use that feature to our advantage

Open the Canva design you want to work with, in one tab. Then, Open the design from which you want to copy the elements in another tab

Select the elements you want to copy (then press control + C or Command C)

then paste those elements or objects in the design you are currently working on, (using the keyboard shortcut Control + C or Command + C)

I recommend you to try it, I find it handy to reuse certain elements of design without having to duplicate the design fully.

Using paid templates, legally

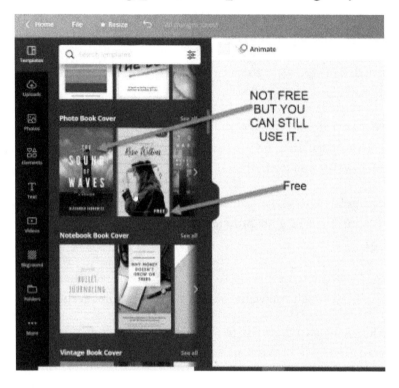

In Canva, you can notice that some templates are labeled as free and some other templates are not labeled so. Did you know that you could still use that template?

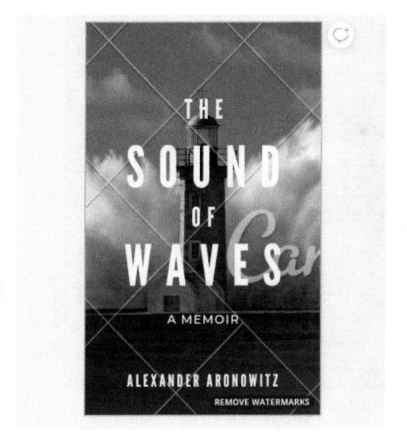

Select a template which is not marked as free, and it will be displayed in your Canvas (the white area)

You will see a watermark in the image, and you cannot use it for free

But wait!

Now just find a different image that is copyright free, from the photos tab or upload your own image. (I have uploaded my own image in this example)

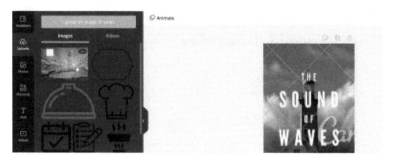

Now drag the image and drop it into the existing copyrighted image (to replace that image with your own image. (As shown in the GIF image above)

Now you have a design which you can use for free, and it is totally legal.

Applying Custom fonts to text

One of the important features of Canva pro is that you can upload your own fonts in Canva and work with them in your designs. This is a very useful feature for designers.

If you still cannot afford a Canva pro (and your trial has expired) then we must find a workaround to this feature.

I warn you that this workaround is not as comfortable as working with Canva pro if you have already worked with Canva pro, but you cannot afford it anymore.

Let me be honest here.

I found a workaround for it which is a little lengthy, but I feel it is worth it if you want to make your designs unique with the use of custom fonts.

Let's do it!

To search for a font in Canva, add a text then change its font, you will find the font menu.

You can also use this shortcut key to Open the font menu: Shift + Control / Command + F

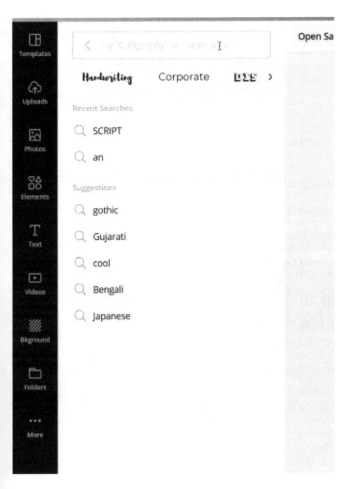

CANVA TIPS AND TRICKS BEYOND THE LIMITS

Search for the font you want to use in Canva by typing the font's name in the font search box

If you don't find the font, then you can use the workaround

Things you will need

Photoshop/ GIMP (it's free)

The font

Make sure you have already installed the font on PC or MAC.

Open Photoshop or Gimp.

For demonstration, I am using Photoshop here

Create a new file with appropriate dimensions that would be required to fit in the text

Add text to it using the type tool and apply the font

After typing the text, double-click the 'T' near the text layer to select the text and then apply the font, size, and other properties

Double-click the text layer and apply any layer style to it (optional)

Apply any additional styles you want to (optional step)

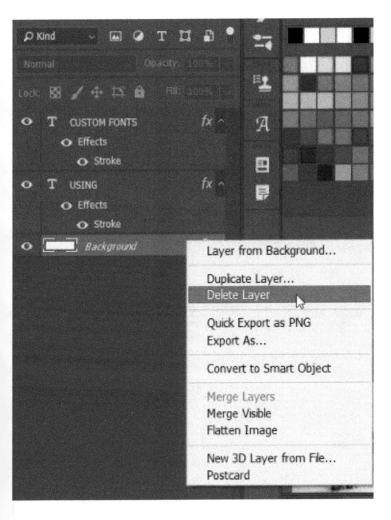

Delete the background layer (Important)

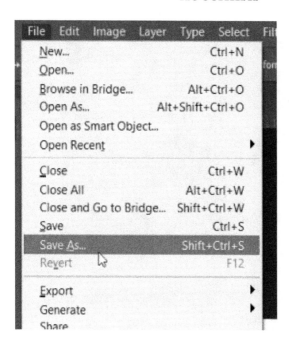

Click Save as from the file menu

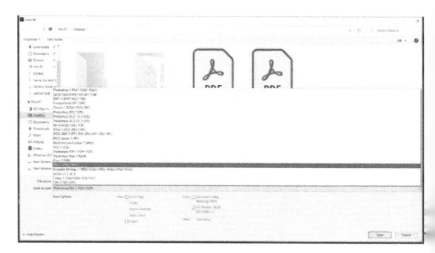

Save the file as PNG/SVG format (with transparency)

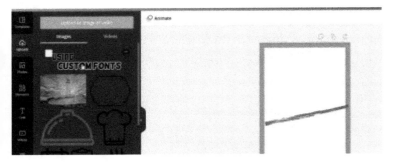

Upload the PNG/SVG file in Canva and add it to your design.

resize the image as required by dragging the white circles in the corner.

Note: SVG files can be resized as per requirement without getting it blurry.

Tip: if you are planning to use a PNG, increase or decrease the font size in Photoshop/GIMP before exporting for better results.

Note: this may sound like too much work to you but in my experience, this won't take a lot of time even if you want to use 2-3 fonts per design (which are not available in Canva for free users.)

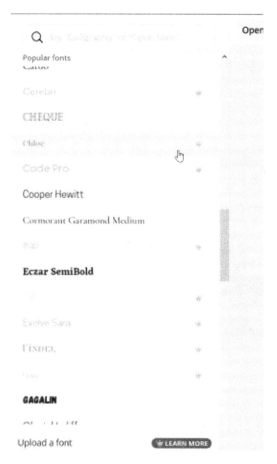

An Extra Tip: you can also search for fonts available only in the pro version, and you can see if you already have it with the correct license. In that case, you can use this technique to use that font

Making GIF Animations without Canva pro version but with the help of Canva

There is a beautiful feature of Canva called Canva animator/ Canva animate, which is available only for Canva pro users.

However, we have a workaround to use Canva to design GIF animations by designing the animations using Canva and then using another powerful software, which is also free.

Things you will need

1. Canva

2. Openshot video editor (only for advance control)

https://www.openshot.org/download/

Click the link above and download it. We will use it in the latter part of this section.

Let's start with the animation.

Open Canva.com

Click create design and select any dimensions you want. For this example, let me select an Instagram post

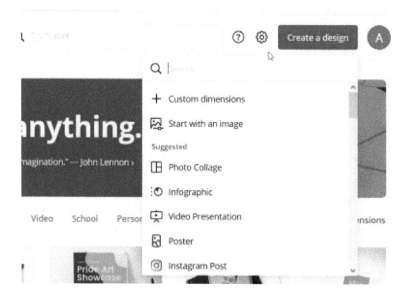

Now search for an element to use in animation. For the sake of this example, I will search for an idea bulb with light rays. Double-click the element to insert it into the page.

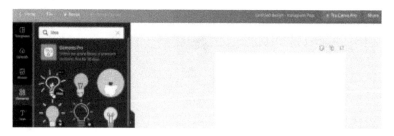

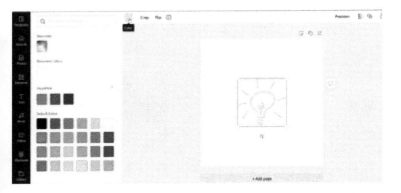

Click the color box and change the color to something you want. (I am changing the color of the idea bulb to yellow, for better visibility.)

Now search for a square shape and click on it to insert it into the design

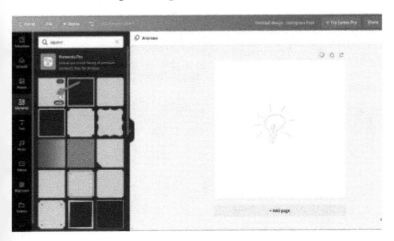

Change the color of the square to white.

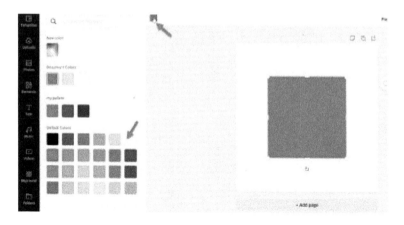

Resize the square to hide one of the light rays (as shown below)

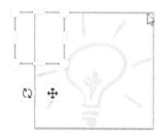

Copy the square by selecting the square and pressing CONTROL + C and paste the square Pressing CONTROL+V and hide all the light rays, as shown below.

Now click the duplicate button and duplicate the page

Delete one square and duplicate the page to create a new page

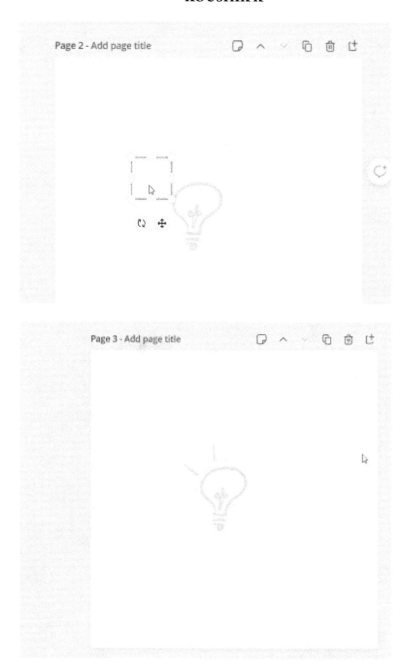

Delete another square on the new page, and then duplicate it,

Continue doing this until all the squares are deleted.

Click on the duplicate page button,

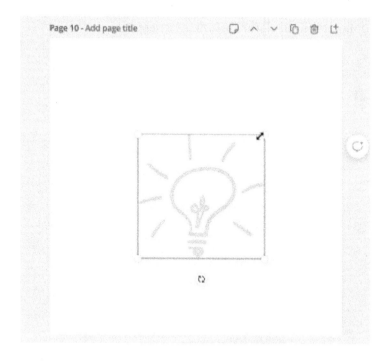

Click on the bulb and drag the comers to resize it a little

Then click the duplicate button

Continue this step again a few times

When you are finally satisfied with the size of the bulb. Click on the bulb image, then, click on the color box and select green (or any other color you want)

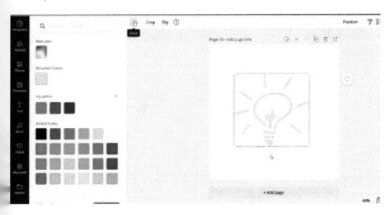

Click the duplicate page button

Then click the text, and then click any text effect to add it.

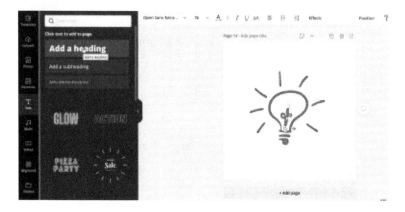

For this example, I will be using the GLOW effect

change the text color to green. then type the letter 'I' then duplicate the page

Add the letter 'D' to the text box on the new page, then duplicate the page again

Add the letter 'E' to the text box, then duplicate the page again

Finally, add the letter 'A' to the text box on the new (duplicated) page

CANVA TIPS AND TRICKS BEYOND THE LIMITS

Now the animation is complete, the next step is to export all the images as a combined PDF from Canva.

Press download, select PDF Standard under file type from the drop-down

Click download button

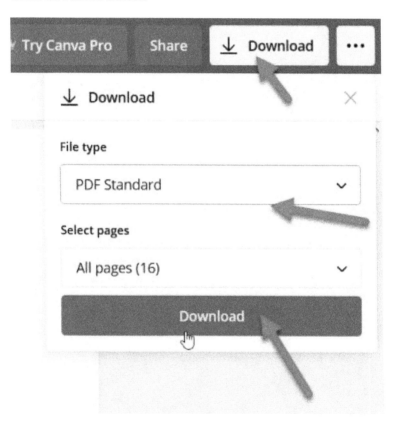

Converting the PDF file to GIF File

Visit **https://ezgif.com/pdf-to-gif**

Click browse, file open dialog box will be displayed. Select the PDF file you want to upload and click open. Then press the upload button

Wait for it to be uploaded and in a few seconds or minutes, depending upon the file size, you will see the screen shown below, check the 'Create animated GIF' checkbox

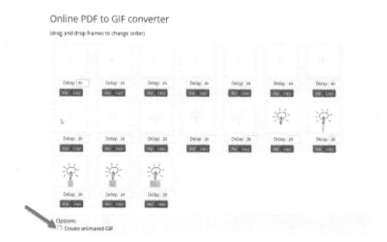

Scroll down a little and click convert to GIF

Wait for a few seconds and a preview of your GIF file will be displayed on the screen, scroll down a little and click save.

For more advanced control over the animation, for adding sound, etc. (MP4 Video Output) you will need a more complicated software

Openshot is a free video editor which can be used for those kinds of needs

Installing openshot

Download openshot from

https://www.openshot.org/download/

if you haven't already downloaded

open the and start the installation

Select the language you want and click OK

Click I accept the agreement and then click next

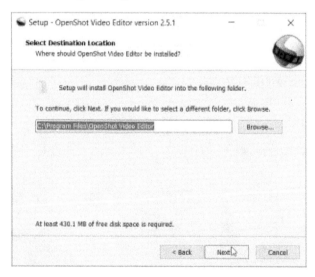

Select the directory you want the software to be installed in and then click Next.

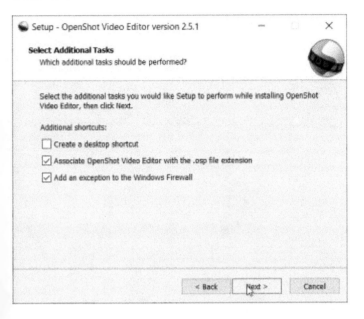

Click next again

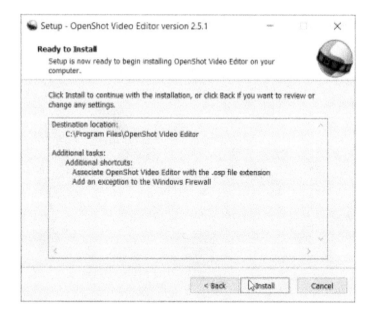

Click install

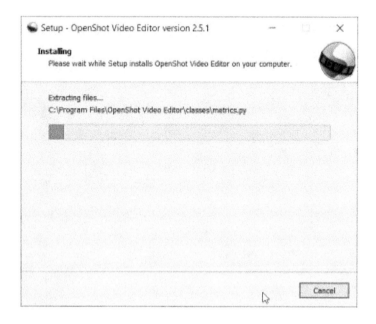

Just wait for a while until it completes

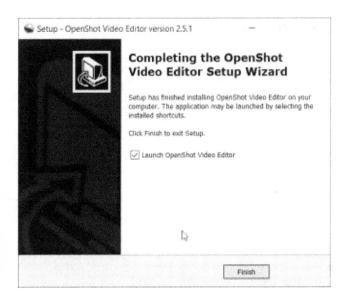

Click Finish

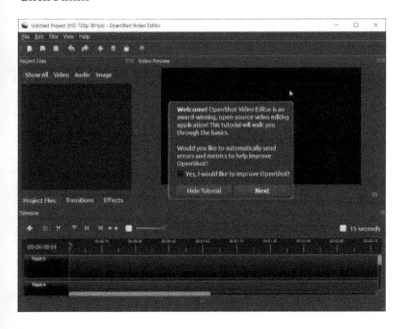

The application opens, click hide tutorial.

Downloading the design from Canva

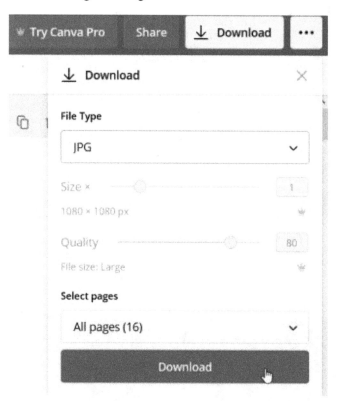

Click the download button in the top right corner, a screen pops up with all the options, select JPG then select All pages and click the download button below.

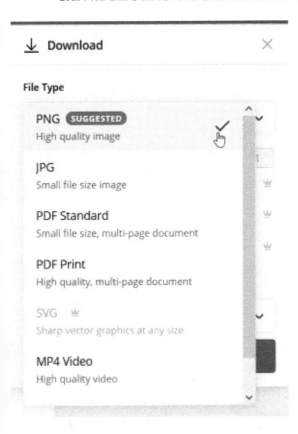

You also have other options like PNG, (if you want to try) (optional)

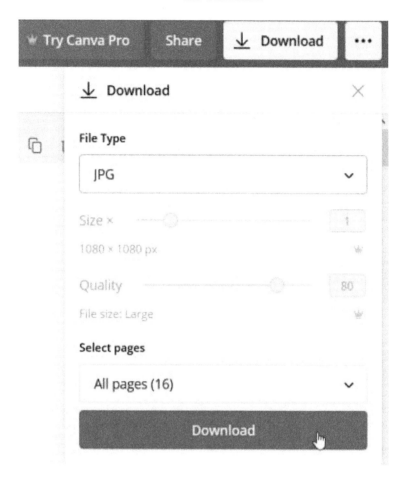

I am just selecting JPG for this example

Click the download button below (the violet one) after selecting your preferred options.

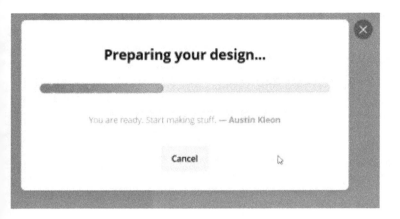

The screen shown above pops up, just wait

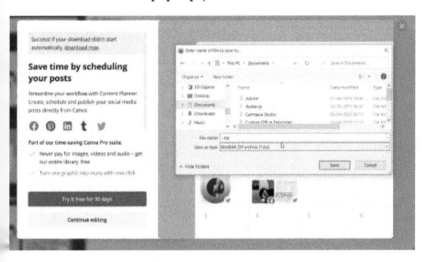

Save file dialog box popup up, just save it in your desired folder.

Unzip that file to a folder, now you are ready to import your files to open shot

Importing files to openshot

Open openshot

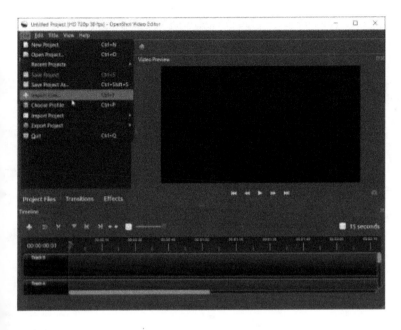

Click the file menu, then select import files.

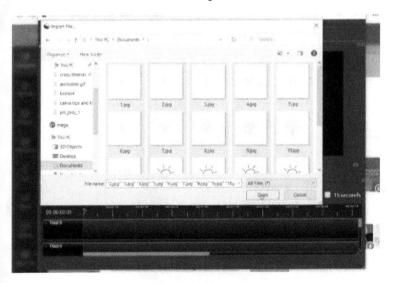

Select all the images to be imported from the folder and click Open.

Click the no button, in the message box that pops up

Repeat the same step until all the images are imported

After all the images are imported, click the edit menu, then click preferences from the drop-down.

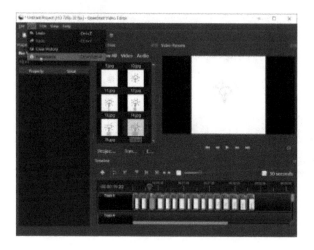

The preferences window will pop up

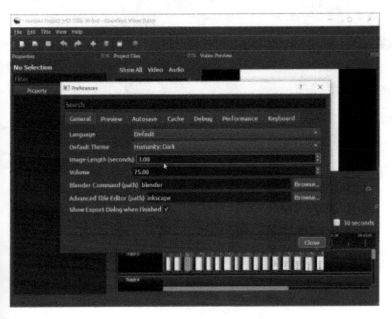

Now change the image length to your need.

What is image length?

Image length is the length of time the image will be shown in the animation timeline by default when they are inserted

For my animation, which has 16 images, and I want my animation to be of 32 – 25 seconds, then I would want my images to be shown for 2 seconds each

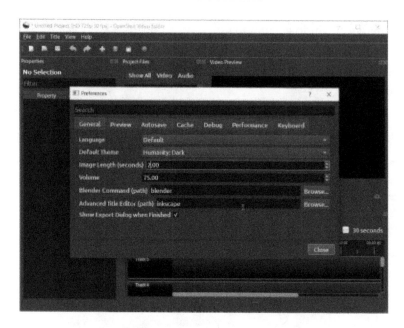

Now click close and, start placing the images in the timeline

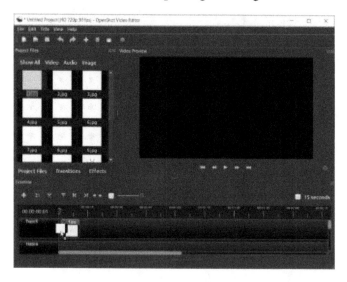

Click and drag the image and drop it in the topmost track, one by one (in the correct order)

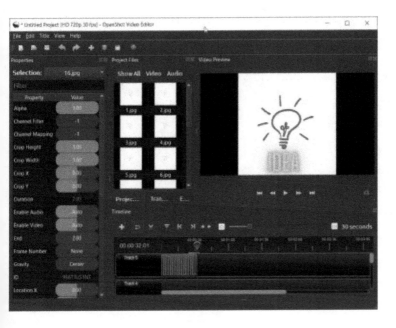

After adding all the images to the track timeline, you can click the play button to preview the animation

If you feel the animation is too slow or too fast, you can adjust the length of every frame by clicking on the right or left side and dragging it.

Then by clicking in the center of the frame and pulling it nearer or farther.

Adding sound to the animation

Import any suitable background music or audio you wish to add to the animation (following the same steps you used to import the images)

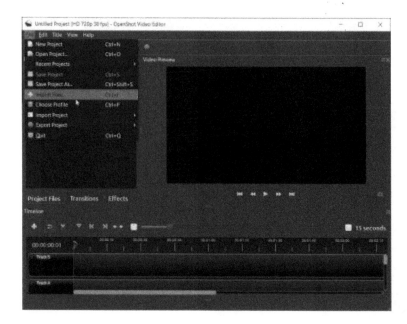

File>import files

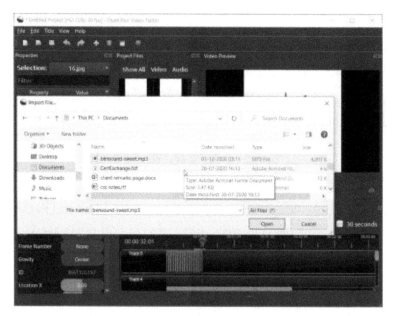

Select the sound file (mp3) then click open

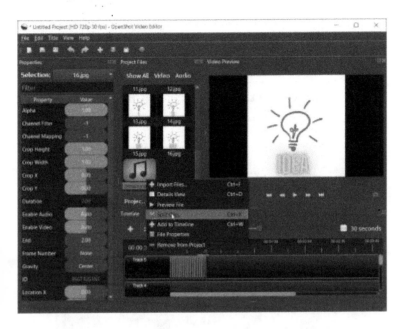

Right-click on the imported sound file and click "split clip"

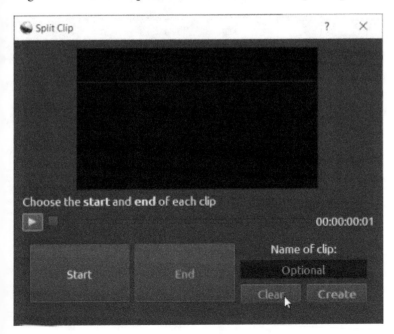

The split clip window opens.

Click play to listen to the clip

Then select the start point of the new clip by pressing start

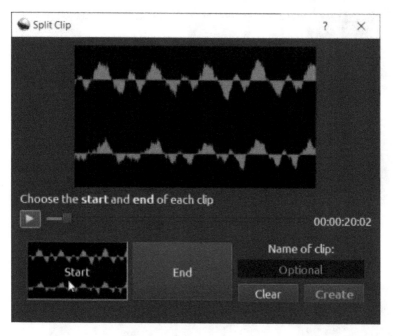

For this example, I am starting the new clip at 00:20:02 of the old clip (by pressing the start button)

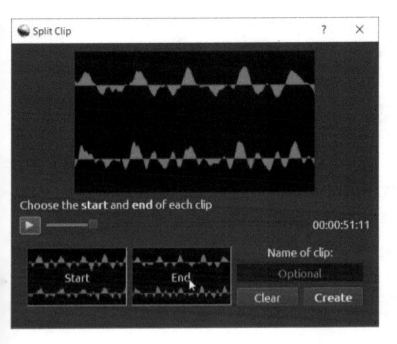

Play the clip further and select your new sound clip's end by pressing the end button.

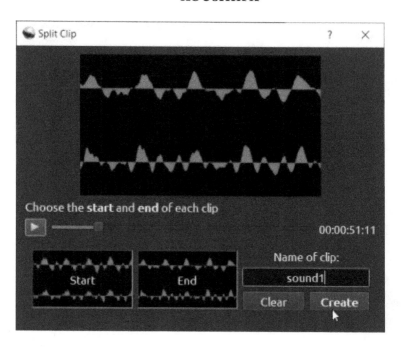

Type in a name for your new clip and click create and then close the spit clip window by pressing the 'x' button at the top

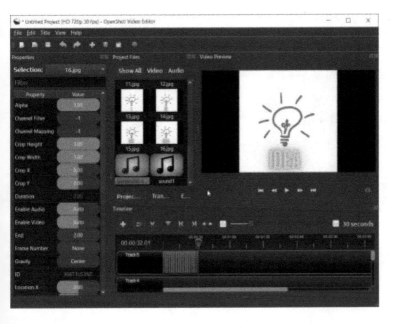

The newly created clip sound 1 will be found in the project files view

Click and drag sound1 file and drop it to track 4's timeline (as shown below)

Now preview the animation, and you will hear the sound along with the animation

Export your animation

File>Export Project> Export Video

An alternative to magic resize

Photoenlarger.com

Step 1: Visit https://www.photoenlarger.com and click the browse button. The file upload dialog box will be displayed.

Step 2: Select the image you want to scale, by clicking on it, then press Open button.

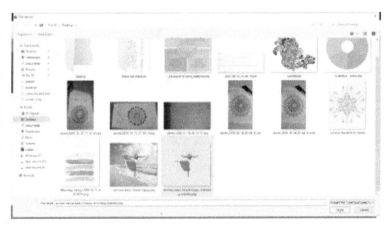

Step 3: select 'enlargement factor' by dragging the slider, or by typing the percentage in the 'scale' text box and Then click enlarge.

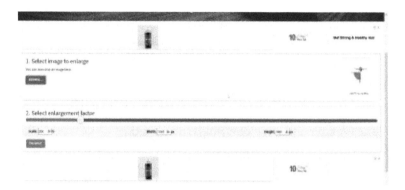

Step 4: then the website will display previews of output from four different enlargement algorithms. Choose the best one, which suits the image. (There is no standard recommendation because different algorithm works better for different images)

Step 5: click the blue download button to download the output of any preview you are satisfied with.

Step 6: the download button gives you two opens, click on PNG for transparent images, click on JPG for images without transparency

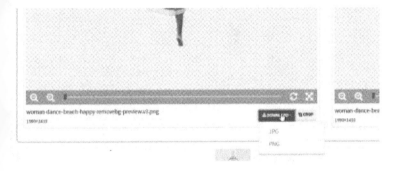

The output of the image I downloaded (just for demo purposes)

A sharper scaling (free software available for desktop)

In my experience, this is the best software available for upscaling the images

Download this free software for windows from the below link

http://a-sharper-scaling.com/#download

Click the download button, save it to your desktop and install the software following the steps

step 1:

Search for a sharper scaling from the start menu, then click open

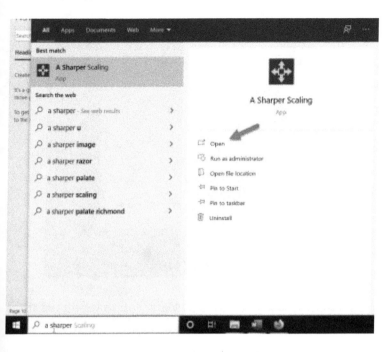

Step 2: click the folder icon; the file open dialog box will appear. Select the file you want to open

Step 3: Select the file you want to open and click the open button

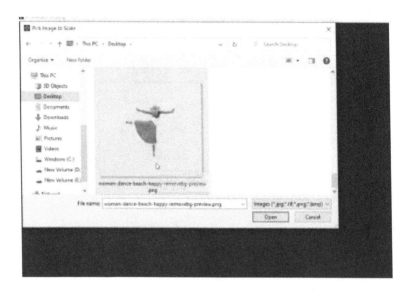

Step 4: crop the image if needed, by clicking and dragging the small white squares on the sides of the frame (optional)

Step 5: once you drag the squares, the frame will become smaller. (in this example, I am just cropping the extra transparent background, but you can also crop a part of the image if needed.

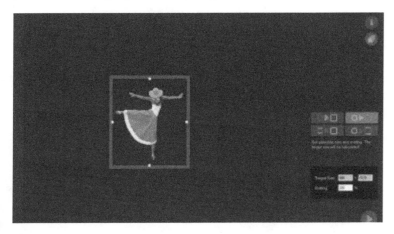

Step 6: change the scaling percentage if required and click the play button. (I recommend up to 200 % and not more than that, to preserve image quality. Though the software allows you to scale it up to 400 percent.)

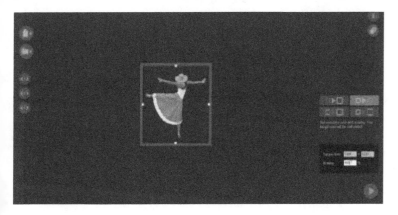

Step 7: a save dialog box will be displayed, just browse to wherever you would like to save the file, type in a name and press save.

Resize images to multiple sizes

Photoresizer.com

Sometimes you need to give the exact dimensions of the image and resize it,

In my personal experience, this website works the best for it.

Go to photoresizer.com

Step1

Click the browse button shown on the website

Step 2

A file open dialog box opens, select the file you want to resize, and press open

Step 3:

Click resize, and then enter the dimensions to which the Image should be resized and press Apply

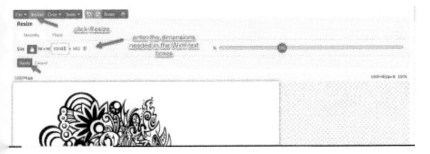

Step 4:

Right-click the output image and select save image as and save it to your desired location

CANVA TIPS AND TRICKS BEYOND THE LIMITS

Custom sizes list for different social media designs

This is just a guideline and not an exact size recommendation

- Facebook **profile photo size:**

For desktop: More than or equal to 180 x 180 pixels

For mobile: More than or equal to 140 x 140 pixels

- Facebook **banner dimensions:** 1200 x 630 pixels

- Link/ **Update image size:** 1200 x 628 pixels

  - **Facebook event cover image size:** 1200 x 628 pixels
  - **Facebook groups cover photo size**
    For desktop: 1640 x 662 pixels
    For mobile: 1640 x 859 pixels

- Twitter **profile picture size:** 400 x 400 pixels (file size must be less than 2 MB)

- Twitter **cover photo size:** 1500 x 500 pixels (file size must be less than 5 MB)

- Shared **image:** 900 x 450 pixels

- In-**stream photo size:** 440 x 220 pixels

LinkedIn Image Sizes

Personal profile:

Profile photo: 400 x 400 pixels

Cover image: 1584 x 396 pixels

- Company **page:**

Logo size: 300 x 300 pixels (min); 400 x 400 pixels (max); File size: 4 MB (max)

Cover image: 1584 x 768 pixels

- Blog **post image:** 1350 x 440 pixels

- Profile **image:** 165 x 165 pixels

- Pin **size:** 236 pixels x Adjustable Height; 2:3 ratio for vertical pins (recommended)

- Board **image size:** 222 x 150 pixels

Instagram Image Sizes

- Profile **photo size:** 110 x 110 pixels

- Photo **size:** 1080 x 1080 pixels

- Photo **thumbnail:** 161 x 161 pixels

Instagram reel size

9:16 (1080 X 1920)

YouTube Image sizes

- **Channel cover photo:** 2560 x 1440 pixels
- **Channel icon:** 800 x 800 pixels
- **Video uploads:** 16:9 ratio
  With the fixed ratio, you can upload your video in various resolutions, such as;
  4K – 3840 x 2160 pixels

CANVA TIPS AND TRICKS BEYOND THE LIMITS

2K –2560 x 1440 pixels
1080p (HD) – 1920 x 1080 pixels
720p (HD) – 1280 x 720 pixels
480p –854 x 480 pixels
360p –640 x 360 pixels
240p –426 x 240 pixels
144p –256 x 144 pixels

Brand Kit

This section of Canva gives many features, for Canva pro users (paid version of Canva)

You can access it on the left side menu (in Canva home)

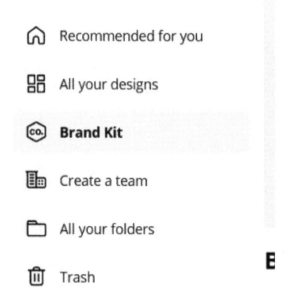

Brand Logo

You can upload the logos which you use commonly here (Pro only feature)

Brand color

Canva free version only allows you to save 1 color palette and only three different color swatches, but in the pro version you can have multiple palettes (which is really handy)

You can rename your palette by double-clicking on the name untitled and deleting it, and then typing there. However, you cannot add a new palette in the free Canva.

You can add up to three colors to your palette by clicking the plus sign

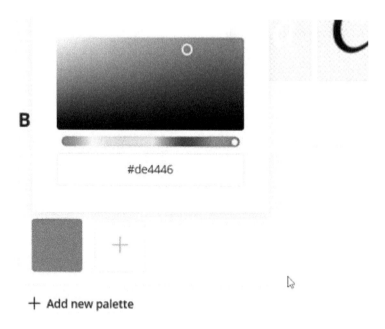

#de4446

+ Add new palette

Select a color or type a color code and press enter to add it.

Brand colors

my pallete   ...

+ Add new palette

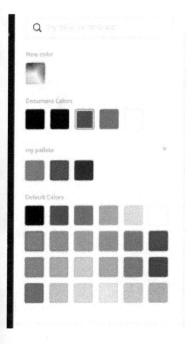

In Canva, you will find the palette whenever you change color to text or images.

You can always change the existing three colors by accessing the brand kit and changing the color again by clicking on the color and selecting a different color.

Brand fonts

You can set font style like font name, font size, and (bold/italic) for Heading, subheading, and body Text

You can upload custom fonts

if you are using a free account of Canva, we need to use some workarounds only, mainly for custom fonts and optionally for brand colors also.

More free Photos and backgrounds

Step 1: click more, you will see different apps; you can scroll to see more of them.

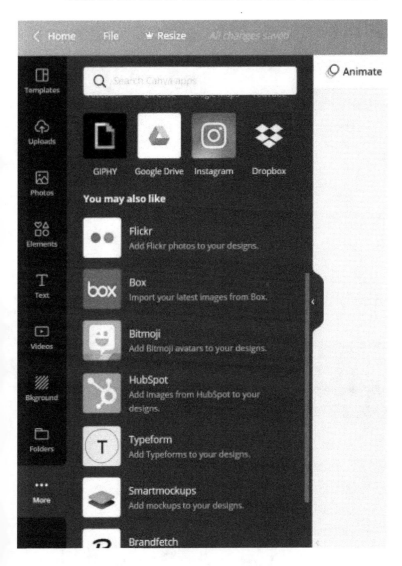

Step 2: add the apps of your choice by clicking them

Step 3: just in some apps, you will get the screen shown below after clicking the app.

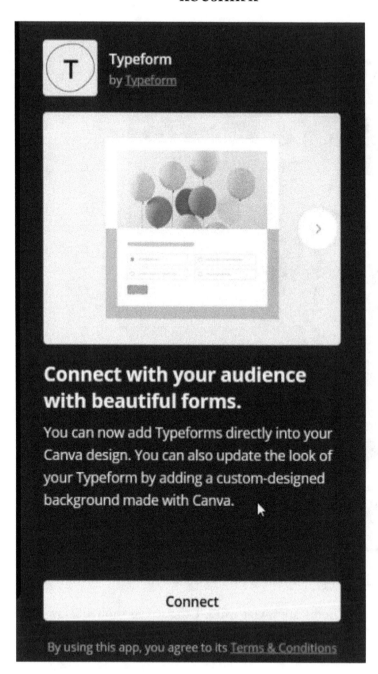

You just need to click connect

Then you can happily start using them

You will find these app tabs on the left corners' slider menu, just below the other default tabs.

Choosing colors from photos

Did you know you can extract all the colors used in a photo? This is a unique and useful feature of Canva. This feature comes in handy to do any brand or logo-based designs. In this chapter, let me show you how to use this neat feature.

Open Canva and choose any template to work with. for this example, I chose to work with the dog poster

After selecting the template, click on any part of the screen with the background color, It will open the colors panel (see the screenshot above)

You will see a background color color-picker box showing the main background color. Click on it

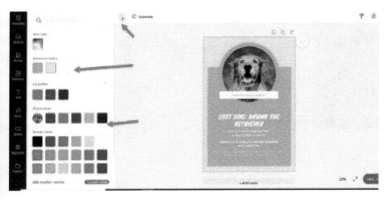

The Color panel will be displayed. There will be different sections showing different collections of colors.

Document colors show all the colors used in the document (background colors, font colors, etc.)

Photo colors show the colors used in the photo (in this example the dog photo)

If the design has multiple photos, then the colors used in each photo are displayed in a separate row, with a small image of that photo on the left.

Now you can apply those photo colors to any element in the design.

This feature is also available for any image you upload

Upload any image you want to extract colors from and add it to the page

Click anywhere on the background of the page, then click on the background-color color picker box

The photo colors of the image, on the page, can be seen in the color panel.

Note: you can also add multiple images you uploaded to a page (as shown below)

CANVA TIPS AND TRICKS BEYOND THE LIMITS

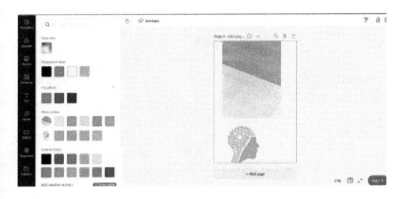

Styles

There is a really useful feature in Canva which is given as an optional tab inside more. Tab

Open Canva

Scroll down the tabs and find more, then click it,

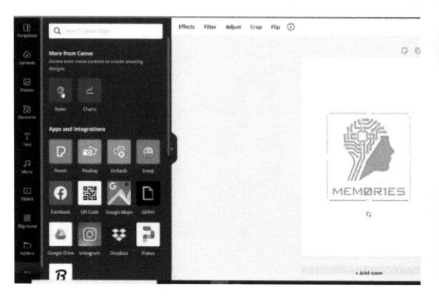

Then click styles

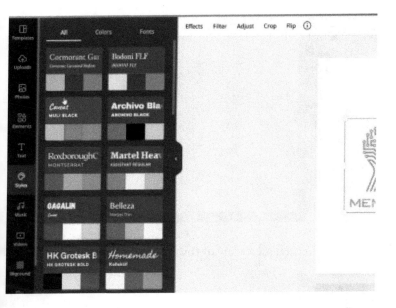

Styles tab will be added to Canva, below the text tab

Select any template you want to work on, for this example, I will be using this dog poster template

Click on 'style tab', then select any of the color and font presets given

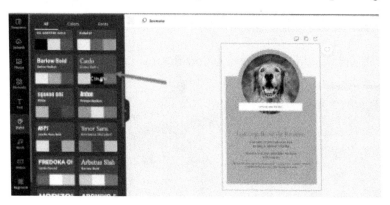

For this example, I clicked the style preset as shown above (and you can see that the colors and fonts of the template changed according to the selected preset.

Now, if you want to change the colors without changing the font selection, you can click on the colors tab inside the styles, and try different colors

To change the fonts alone and retain the original colors of the template, click on any font presets inside the fonts tab of the Styles panel.

Some Tips Regarding Text

Open Canva

Click the text tab in the side panel, to open it

Click any text from the panel to add to the page

Click on the text box added to your design to edit the text.

Type any text and to add an effect to it select the text and then click the effect button

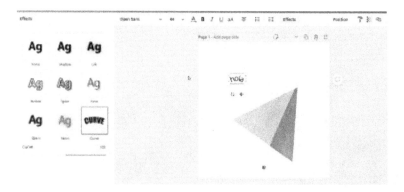

Effect panel will appear in left

Click on any effect you want to apply.

Copying the style of one text to another text

Select the text you want to copy the style from

Then click copy style icon in the text toolbar that appears on the top

Click any text in which you want to paste the style

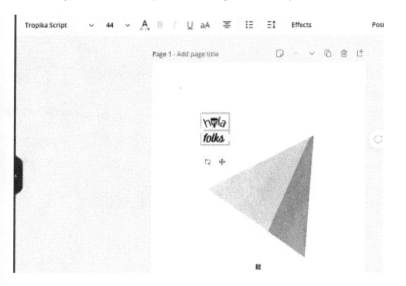

Now you can see that the other text also changes to the same style (font, color size, etc.)

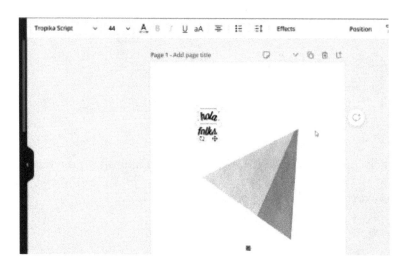

Frames

Frames are nothing but image containers in different shapes, they can be used in a number of creative ways

Open Canva,

Create a new design or open your existing design you want to work on

Click elements

Then in the search box type frames and hit enter

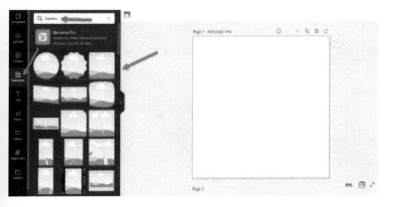

Click on a frame you like to insert it

Now go to uploads, upload an image and then drag the image and drop it into the frame

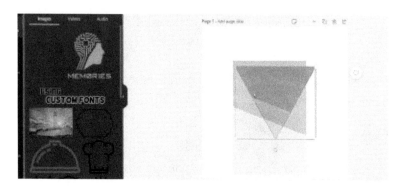

See what happens

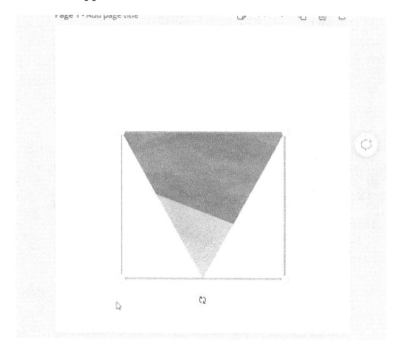

Now your image is masked with the shape of the frame

You can double-click the frame and adjust the image by clicking and dragging the white circle handles in the corners or by moving around by dragging, clicking, and dragging from the center

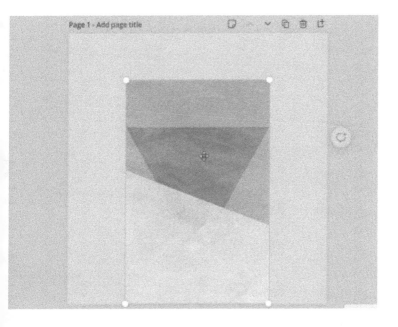

Press enter key after you have finished adjusting

Now you can select this framed image and resize it by dragging the white dots (circles) in the corners

Rotate by clicking and dragging the rotating arrows handle like any other image

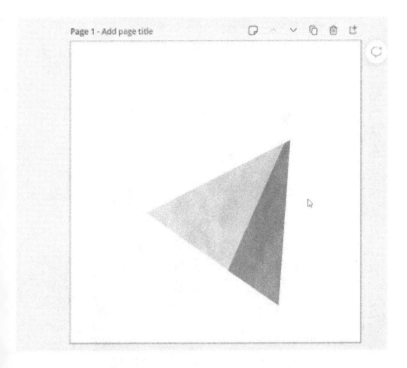

If you go to elements then search frames and scroll down you can find frames in the shape of every alphabet, which is highly useful for title designs

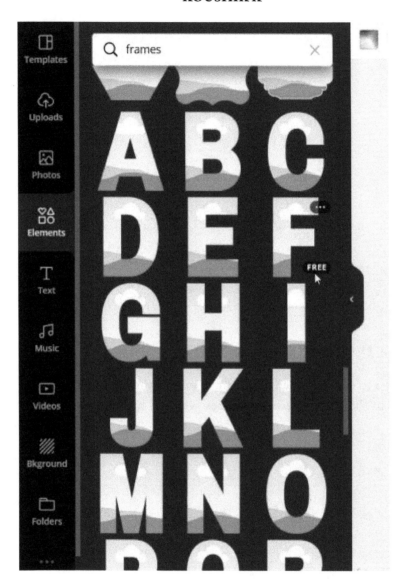

You can also combine multiple frames by keeping them near and creating many designs, the possibilities are endless.

Keywords for searching inside Canva

Some keywords to search inside the photos tab to find cool stuff to add to your design

Open Canva

Click the photos tab

Type in one of the keywords listed below and see what you find

Brush strokes

Paint stokes

Torn paper

Paper

Frames

Polaroid

Gold+metallic+brushstroke

Metallic

Brushstroke

Glitter

Abstract

Grunge

Gradient

Wood

Marble

Splash

Sparkles

Illustration

Ripped frame

Borders

texture

Keywords to search inside elements tab of Canva

line drawing

illustration

shapes

drawing

icon

pattern

dots

silhouette

neon

brush

watercolor

blob

CANVA TIPS AND TRICKS BEYOND THE LIMITS

freeform

ripped frame

collage

calligraphy

swoosh

sparkle

glitters

geometric

drops

wave

Folders without Folders

Canva offers a feature called folders, you can organize your designs in various folders, categories, and you can create many folders as you want if you are using Canva Pro.

Now, what if you are using Canva Free Version.

You can only create 2 custom folders, if that's enough for you to organize your designs, then you are done.

If you want to organize your designs into more categories, please read further.

You may know that you can search all your designs (using your browsers search facility)

control + F or Command + F

I use Firefox

If you start naming your design with your category as your first word in the design title, you can easily find them by type. So that you don't have to scroll through every design.

I know this is not a proper folder, but this still solves your purpose a little by helping you organize your stuff the way you want (without having to pay anything!)

See the screenshot below, you can understand how it works

CANVA TIPS AND TRICKS BEYOND THE LIMITS

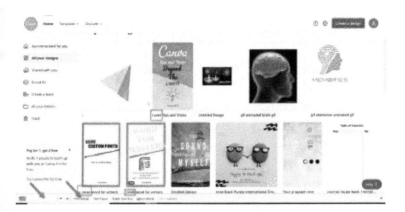

Exporting images in 300 DPI (Images for High-Quality Print)

There are three steps involved in preparing a digital image for print.

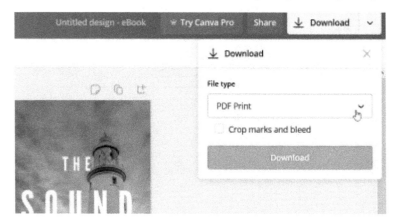

Step 1:

The only way to download a high-quality print-ready image in Canva is to download a Pint quality PDF from Canva.

1. click download

2. Select PDF Print from the drop-down menu

3. Click the blue download button,

Step 2:

Then you can convert the PDF into a high-quality JPG

1. Visit https://pdf2jpg.net

2. Click 'choose a PDF file' button and upload the PDF you want to convert

3. Select Excellent – 300 DPI Rich Illustrations, High-Quality JPEG from the drop-down menu

Step 3:

Then you will have to convert the color scheme from RGB (which is the best scheme for digital screens) to CMYK (which is the color scheme used for print.)

Visit https://rgb2cymk.org

Click browse and upload the JPEG you got from pdf2jpg.net

Leave everything else as default, and then click start

Making Landing pages and Websites with Canva

We all need websites or landing pages for various purposes, for promoting products or services or for building a portfolio or bio.

Do you know, Canva offers us a great feature for making such websites?

Let us discuss that feature now

We all know what static websites or basic landing pages are made of.

Just design elements and links. As you may already know, in Canva you can create links using a text or design elements (shapes images, etc.)

Note: The hyperlinks you create in Canva are functional when you download a PDF of the design.

Now we are going to see how to use those designs as websites or landing pages (and not just PDFS)

Create a blank design in Canva with the dimensions of your choice

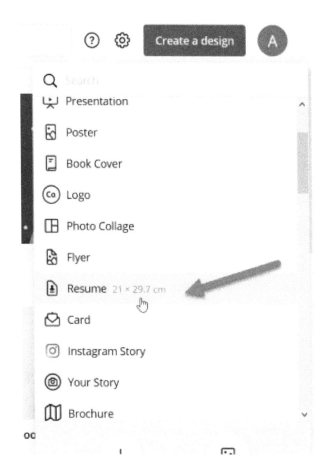

For this example, I am using a 21x29.7 cm resume dimension

Open the templates tab and search for a template, I am searching for a template with a headshot photo to create an author bio

Search for a bio template, landing page template, or Instagram bio template according to your need

Then start designing and customizing the page

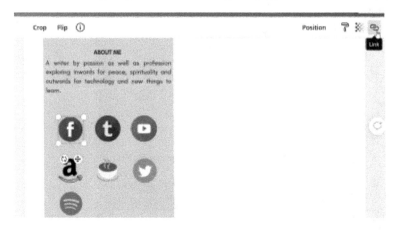

I have created an about me text, added images for social websites

Click the image of the social icon, then click the link icon to add a hyperlink

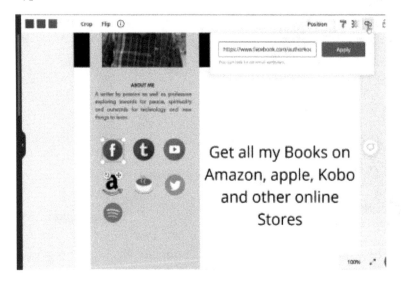

Type in the URL (web address) and then click apply

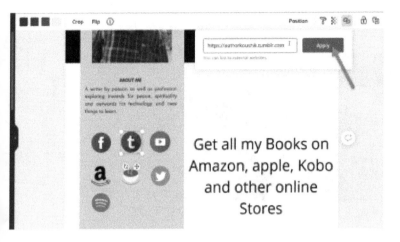

Repeat the steps for all the icons you want to link

To add links to text boxes, click the three horizontal dots and then click the link icon, type in the address, and click apply. (just like you have done before with the images)

After completing the design, now we will start building the landing page or website

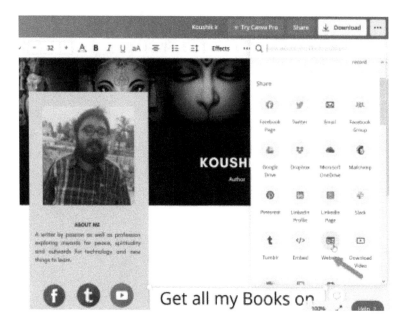

Click the three horizontal dots button, then click the website icon (as shown above)

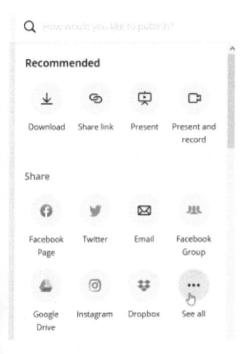

Note: If the website icon is not shown, click the see all icon and scroll to find the website icon

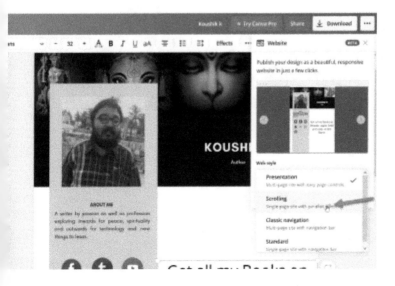

In the web style drop-down box, select scrolling

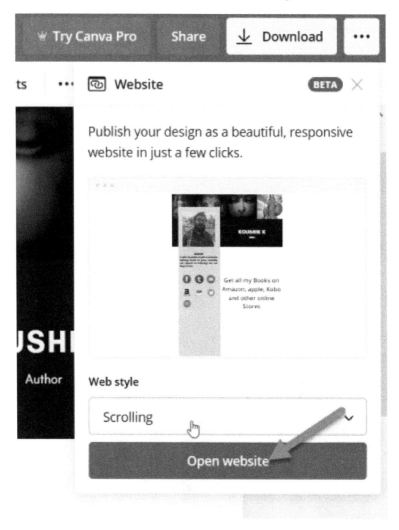

Then click open website

A website opens in a new tab (that is your newly built/ website or landing page) which you built easily within just a few minutes.

Just select the address shown in the address bar and copy it, paste it in a notepad or any safe place.

Now you can share this link with anyone, on any web page, or social media. Canva will store this page permanently on their servers.

Disadvantages of Landing pages of websites designed in Canva

1. It is not responsive: a page designed in a particular dimension for desktop computers does not fit for the mobile. Viewers, so that can be seen as the biggest disadvantage the era is of responsive design
2. When we click the links, Canva displays a warning which in my opinion can turn down many views and clicks

You are about to leave Canva

https://authorkoushik.tumblr.com is an external website that isn't affiliated with Canva.

Double-check the link before continuing.

Continue to external site

Suspicious of this website?
If it doesn't seem right, report it.

Report link

3. At the time of writing this guide (Feb 2021), Canva does not offer the feature of having a custom domain/ custom URL for landing pages.

Making Resumes in Canva

We can create different kinds of designs in Canva, be it presentations, Instagram posts, Facebook covers, Facebook posts, e-book covers, etc.

One of such designs is 'resume', in this chapter, I want to discuss about making resumes in Canva.

In Canva, you can make all kinds of resumes, for all kinds of professions and what I like best about resumes in Canva is their articles by experts advising what kind of resume template will be suitable for which type of professionals.

That becomes a really useful treasure-like advice for a fresher

Open Canva

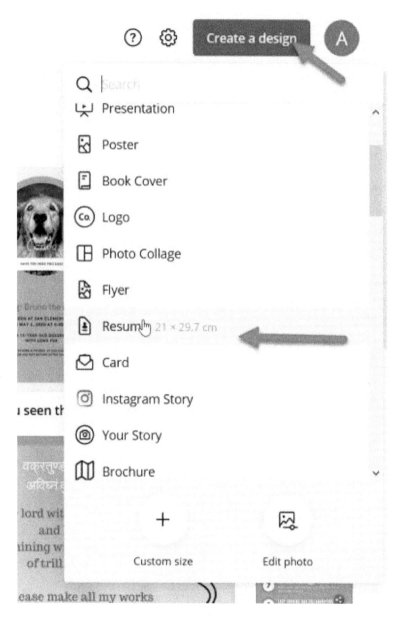

Click create design and select 'resume'

Click templates and open the templates tab and search for 'your profession' resume

Example: web designer resume (as shown above)

Example: Architect resume (shown above)

You can also search "Canva resumes" in google and find nice advice on what kind of resume template to use for your profile and profession

You can read those recommendations

For example, visit this article from the below link

https://www.Canva.com/learn/professional-resume-template/[1]

Read the recommendations

If you like a template, then click the 'use this template' button below the template image

---

1. https://www.canva.com/learn/professional-resume-template/

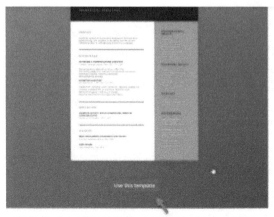

How it works: The clean, straightforward layout of this resume is professional enough for even the most conservative jobs, industries, or companies—but the color blocking adds enough visual interest to keep it from crossing the line into boring or generic territory.

Then you will be taken to your Canva and there you can customize the design and download it.

Canva Print – bring your designs on flyers and posters

Canva offers you printing services for your designs (Business cards, posters, flyers, etc.) the print is of high quality. Sometimes you get it for a really good price.

I feel that because the design is created in Canva, using their printing services also gives the optimal output.

Log in to Canva and open a design you have already created

Check and confirm if the design is final, (any edit after ordering the prints will not reflect in the printed copies)

CANVA TIPS AND TRICKS BEYOND THE LIMITS

To start the process of ordering print copies, click the three horizontal dots near the download button, then select an option under the heading Print.

For this example, I am going to print a flyer

Most of the options in print are similar, so from this example, you can clearly understand how to print other types of prints too.

The below screen will be displayed on the right side of the design

Now start selecting the options

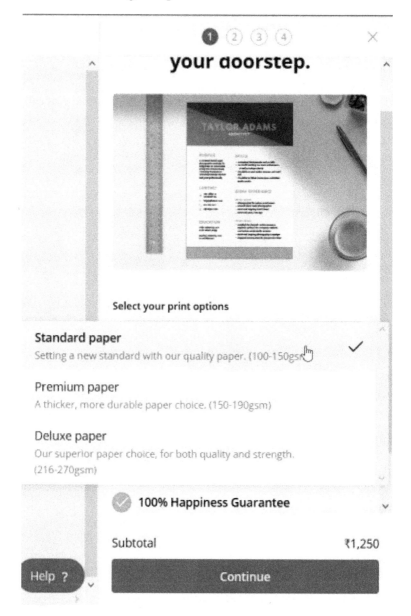

For flyers, 135–170 GSM is the best (you can either choose standard or premium) according to the purpose and use of the flyer

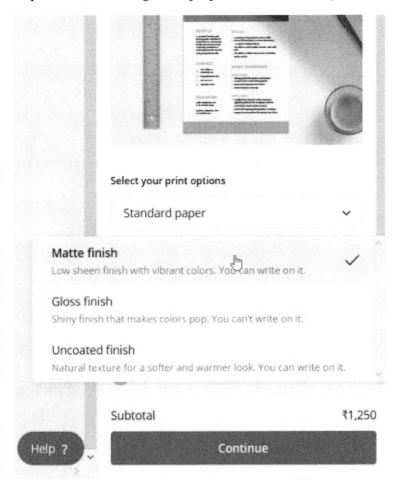

A *gloss* finish is the best for *flyers* with designs and lots of visuals.

If the flyer is made of mostly text and simple designs, matte would be fine.

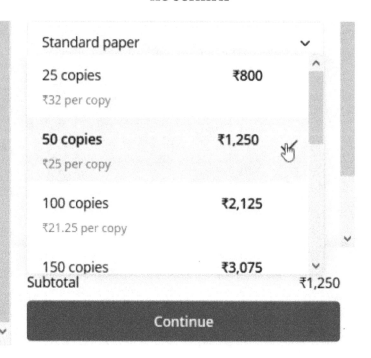

The next thing to choose is the number of copies, each type of print has a minimum order requirement, meaning you will not be able to order 1 copy and test it

Though you can order the minimum number of copies to test it out, be sure to scroll down and check the prices first before deciding the number of copies to order.

Canva will also show you the price per copy charged, which is a useful factor to decide.

In the time of writing this book when scrolled down to see the maximum number of copies, I found something interesting

Please look at the above screenshot, the price for ordering 200 copies, is lesser than ordering 25 copies, it is obvious that I decided to test it by ordering 200 copies rather than 25 copies.

After selecting the options you have decided to, press continue

Do you see any white areas around the edges?

Stretch your background. This way, you won't see any white edges in your prints.

Now Canva will show the above frame, it will start giving you a few tips.

If you have white space in your design in the corners and edges, drag your background image and stretch it.

Now click continue

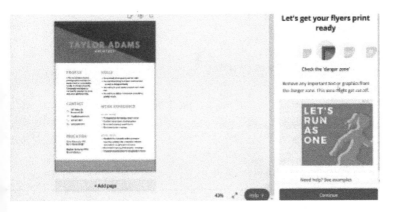

Click if you have any design elements or text in the area marked by red by Canva, in your design, if you see the above design that red area only has background color in my design

Click continue

Now Canva will show you images which is of low quality in your design, those images may not look good in print

All you have to do is change the DPI of that image and upload it back and then use it in the design or use a different High-Quality Image

To change the dpi of the image, just upload that particular image in

https://convert.town/image-dpi

And chose the DPI (as shown below)

300 DPI will be fine for print

Now save the image you got from, https://convert.town/image-dpi on your device,

Upload it to Canva and use it.

Then click the continue button

Canva will now ask you to check your design for spelling and grammar (Canva does not have any built-in spelling and grammar checker, you will have to check it manually)

After checking for Grammatical errors and finalizing the design, click continue

Type in your full name, address, city, and state or province.

Note that you will not be able to change the country.

Click continue

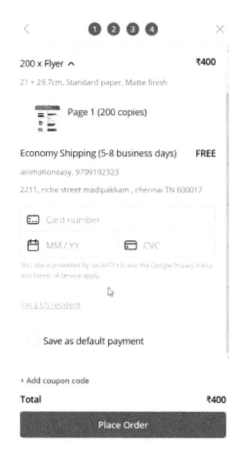

Just fill in your card details and place the order.

Canva Shortcuts

- Select All Elements: **cmd/CTRL** + "**A**" key
- Select Next: Tab
- Select Previous: Shift + Tab
- Add a **line** to your document: Click the "**L**" key
- Add a **rectangle** to your document: Click the "**R**" key
- Add a **Text** to your document: Click the "**T**" key

- Make **Text** Bold: **cmd/CTRL** + "**B**" key
- Make **Text** Italic: **cmd/ CTRL** + "**I**" key
- Transform text to Uppercase: **Shift** + **cmd/CTRL** + "**K**" key
- Add Border to text Alt/ Option + Shift + B
- Increase the size of the border: Alt/ Option + Shift + Equals sign
- Decrease the size of the border: Alt/ Option + Shift + Minus sign
- Send objects or elements forward or backward: Command/ Control) + [or Command/ Control +].
- Send objects to Back or Front: Control / Command + Alt/ Option + [or Control/Command) + Alt/Option +].
- Open font menu: Shift + Control / Command + F
- Increase Font Size: Shift + Control / Command+ equal sign
- Decrease Font Size: Shift + Control / Command+ Minus sign
- Align Text to right: Shift + Control / Command+ R
- Align Text to Left: Shift + Control / Command+ L
- Align Text to Center: Shift + Control / Command+ C
- Anchor Text to Top: Shift + Control / Command+ H
- Anchor Text to middle: Shift + Control/Command + M
- Anchor text to bottom: Shift + Control / Command+ B

- Align text boxes: Shift + Control / Command+ J
- Increase line spacing: alt/Options + Up arrow
- Decrease line spacing: alt/Options + Down Arrow
- Duplicate Object in Control/ Command + D
- Zoom in Control/ Command + equals sign
- Zoom out: Control/ Command + Minus sign
- Zoom to Actual Size: Control/ Command + 0
- Zoom to Fit: Alt/ Option + Control/ Command + 0
- Zoom to Fill: Shift + Control/ Command + 0
- Show/hide grids Command (or Control) + ;
- Undo: Control/ Command + Z
- Redo: Control/ Command + Shift + Z

- To select a hidden element, Hold Control Key and Left Click on it
- To maintain the proportions while resizing hold Shift
- To draw a straight line – hold shift while drawing
- Select multiple objects: Shift + Click
- To nudge around selected elements by 1-pixel, use arrow keys for precise movements
- SHIFT +arrow keys for moving objects in increments

- Group Elements: **cmd/CTRL** + "**G**" key
- Ungroup Elements: **shift** + **cmd/CTRL** + "**G**" key
- Toggle object panel: Control/ Command + /
- Add Empty Page: Control/ Command + Return key
- Delete Empty Page: Control/ Command + Delete key
- Show/hide search: Control / Command+?

SECRET CODE

Type in

brand:BAAAAP7rQ8M

or

brand:BAAMOuJH0Ec

In elements search bar to get only free elements. To me, this is a very useful feature so that I don't get diverted from the free designs.

One warning about this secret code is that I feel not all free elements from Canva are displayed by this.

Canva's Resources

Canva's color tools

https://www.Canva.com/colors/[1]

has four different tools related to color which we can use for free

Coolors.co

https://coolors.co/

Canva's school

https://designschool.Canva.com[2]

learn more about Canva, tips, and tricks for free from Canva. Taking these courses can help you do much more with Canva. (I will also update you with some very useful techniques from time to time)

Get more Design Inspiration

https://www.Canva.com/learn/design-inspiration/[3]

Canva's showcase and tutorials of the best designs can be created with the help of Canva are listed on this page.

---

1. https://www.canva.com/colors/

2. https://designschool.canva.com

3. https://www.canva.com/learn/design-inspiration/

CANVA TIPS AND TRICKS BEYOND THE LIMITS

Illustrations for everyone

https://blush.design

Contact Me:

You can always feel free to contact me or send me suggestions, doubts to writetokoushik@yahoo.com

Follow me at my blog

Authorkoushik.tumblr.com[1]

1. http://authorkoushik.tumblr.com/

Please Leave a Review

Thank you for reading the book. Hope you enjoyed it.

If you like this book and enjoyed reading it, it would be really helpful if you can share your experience by **leaving a review**

If you have had any problems with the book, please feel free to message me through email writetokoushik@yahoo.com

I will try my best to help you with it.

Thank you

Koushik K

Other Books by Author

Tales of Hanuman

Tales of Hanuman vol 2

Hanuman Chalisa Explained

Hanumad Bhujanga Stotra

Rama Raksha Stotra: A Shield Of Rama's Names

The Heart of Sun God - A Hymn from Valmiki Ramayana

The Names of Sun God - A Hymn From Mahabharata

Surya Dvadashanama Stotra - Twelve Names of Sun God

Shadpadee Stotra - A Hymn on Vishnu by Adi Shankaracharya

Achyutashtakam: A Hymn on Lord Vishnu by Adi Shankaracharya

Kali Santarana Upanishad

Narayana Kavacham: From Srimad Bhagavata Purana

Pragyavivardana Stotra - A Hymn from Rudrayamalam: Wisdom Giving Names of Kartikeya Translation Transliteration and Commentary

Durga Saptashloki - The seven verses from Devi Mahathmyam (English)

Durga Saptashloki - The seven verses from Devi Mahathmyam (Tamil)

Durga Chandrakala Stuti: A hymn on Durga by Appayya Deekshita

The Name of Durga: Durga Nama Anushthana

Sarasvati Ashtottara Shatanama Stotra: Hundred and Eight Names of Sarasvati

Rudrashtakam - A Hymn from RamacharitaManas

Shiva Panchakshara Nakshatra Mala - A Hymn on Shiva with 27 Stanzas by Adi Shankara Bhagavadpaada

Shiva Panchakshara Stotra

Shiva Shadakshara Stotra: A Hymn on Shiva's Six Syllable Mantra

Ardhanarishvara Stotra: A Hymn on Unified Form Of Shiva and Shakti by Shankara Bhagavadpaada

Shiva Manasa Pooja: Mental Worship Of Shiva

Kalabhairavashtakam: Eight Verses on Kalabhairava

Hundred and Eight Names of Bhairava

Margabandhu Stotra: A Hymn on Margasahaya Shiva By Appayya Deekshita

Names of Shiva: Commentary on 108 Names of Shiva From Shiva Rahasya Khanda Based on Shiva Tatva Rahasya Of Neelakanta Deekshita

Shiva Namavali Ashtakam An Octet of Shiva's Names By Shankara Bhagavadpaada

Ganesha Pancharatnam: A hymn on Ganesha by Shankara Bhagavadpada

Ganesha Sahasranama - Thousand Names of Ganesha: Translated Based on Bhaskara Raya Makhin's Khadyota Bhashya

Heramba Upanishad

19 PLUS TIPS FOR USING GMAIL TO THE FULLEST

All That You Need To Know About Google Keep for Increasing Productivity

All That You Need to Know When Buying Domains

All That You Need to Know About Tumblr Blogs

Productivity Hacks for Entrepreneurs

Who Should Start a Membership Business

Glories of Shiva: Kaalahastheeshwara (coming soon)

Glories of Shiva: Stories from the Shiva Mahimna Stotra (coming soon)

All books that are published are available through online stores check

authorkoushik.tumblr.com[1]

CPSIA information can be obtained
at www.ICGtesting.com
Printed in the USA
LVHW080759011022
729724LV00029B/1087